# NOT THE

# FILES

## Mapping Public Reports of Unidentified Aerial Phenomena Across America

**MAREK N. POSARD** ▪ **ASHLEY GROMIS** ▪ **MARY LEE**

Prepared for the Office of the Secretary of Defense

Approved for public release; distribution unlimited

RAND | NATIONAL DEFENSE RESEARCH INSTITUTE

For more information on this publication, visit **www.rand.org/t/RRA2475-1**.

**About RAND**

The RAND Corporation is a research organization that develops solutions to public policy challenges to help make communities throughout the world safer and more secure, healthier and more prosperous. RAND is nonprofit, nonpartisan, and committed to the public interest. To learn more about RAND, visit www.rand.org.

**Research Integrity**

Our mission to help improve policy and decisionmaking through research and analysis is enabled through our core values of quality and objectivity and our unwavering commitment to the highest level of integrity and ethical behavior. To help ensure our research and analysis are rigorous, objective, and nonpartisan, we subject our research publications to a robust and exacting quality-assurance process; avoid both the appearance and reality of financial and other conflicts of interest through staff training, project screening, and a policy of mandatory disclosure; and pursue transparency in our research engagements through our commitment to the open publication of our research findings and recommendations, disclosure of the source of funding of published research, and policies to ensure intellectual independence. For more information, visit www.rand.org/about/principles.

RAND's publications do not necessarily reflect the opinions of its research clients and sponsors.

Published by the RAND Corporation, Santa Monica, Calif.
© 2023 RAND Corporation
**RAND®** is a registered trademark.

Library of Congress Cataloging-in-Publication Data is available for this publication.
ISBN: 978-1-9774-1156-3

# About This Report

The U.S. government is responsible for an estimated 5.3 million square miles of domestic airspace and 24 million square miles of oceanic airspace. The February 2023 downing of a Chinese surveillance balloon after it had flown across the country raised questions about the degree to which the U.S. government knows who is flying what over its territorial skies. Like all countries, the United States has finite resources to monitor objects flying through its airspace. At the same time, advances in technology allow the general public, private companies, and civilian government agencies to operate ever-smaller commercially available drones that intentionally or unintentionally capture and contribute to activity in the skies. This trend could make public reports of unidentified aerial phenomena (UAPs) an important source of information for U.S. government officials.

This report presents a geographic analysis of 101,151 public reports of UAP sightings in 12,783 U.S. Census Bureau census designated places. The data were collected by the National UFO Reporting Center (NUFORC), one of the nongovernmental entities that the Federal Aviation Administration has referenced in official documents for where to report unexplained phenomena. The analyses in this report should not be interpreted as an endorsement of any individual report or the overall quality of data that NUFORC has made publicly available. This report provides findings on U.S. locations where UAP reports are significantly more likely to occur and offers recommendations to increase awareness of the types of activities that might be mistaken for unexplained phenomena or that point to potential threats.

The research reported here was completed in May 2023 and underwent security review with the sponsor and the Defense Office of Prepublication and Security Review before public release.

## RAND National Security Research Division

This research was sponsored by the Office of the Secretary of Defense and conducted within the Acquisition and Technology Policy Program of the RAND National Security Research Division (NSRD), which operates the National Defense Research Institute (NDRI), a federally funded research and development center sponsored by the Office of the Secretary of Defense, the Joint Staff, the Unified Combatant Commands, the Navy, the Marine Corps, the defense agencies, and the defense intelligence enterprise.

For more information on the RAND Acquisition and Technology Policy Program, see www.rand.org/nsrd/atp or contact the director (contact information is provided on the webpage).

## Acknowledgments

We thank Laura Baldwin from the Institute for Defense Analyses (formerly of the RAND Corporation) for her support and insights into the scoping of this project. We also thank Chris Mouton, Josh Becker, Jon Fujiwara, John Hoehn, and Jeremy Russell for their feedback, which informed our analytic approach. We are grateful to Lauren Skrabala, whose dedicated work improved the prose of this report. We thank Michael Kennedy and Denis Agniel at RAND for their early reviews of our research approach. Finally, we thank Gabriel Hassler from RAND, Arie Croitoru from George Mason University, and Christopher Mellon, formerly of the U.S. Department of Defense, for their thoughtful reviews.

# Contents

# Figures and Tables

## Figures

## Tables

# CHAPTER 1

# Introduction

In February 2023, the U.S. Air Force shot down a Chinese surveillance balloon off the coast of South Carolina after it had flown over numerous states.[1] This incident raised questions about the degree to which the U.S. government knows who is flying what across its vast airspace.[2] The United States has an estimated 5.3 million square miles of domestic airspace and 24 million square miles of oceanic airspace.[3] Like all countries, the United States has finite resources to track all objects flying overhead. This may become a concern given that more people, companies, and countries have access to tools of airpower (e.g., commercial drones) and these tools are becoming smaller, cheaper, and more accessible because of technological advances (e.g., micro drones). Put simply, we assume there are more things flying in the sky today than in the past. Against this backdrop, we assume that public reporting of aerial phenomena is an asset that may help government officials identify potential threats. This report examines where people are reporting unidentified aerial phenomena (UAPs) across the United States.

## Motivation for This Research

There has been growing interest among U.S. government, defense, and intelligence organizations about UAPs flying in U.S. airspace.[4] For example, the U.S. Department of Defense (DoD) operated the Advanced Aviation Threat Identification Program between 2007 and 2012 to collect and analyze data on aerospace threats.[5] In 2021, the Office of the Director of

---

[1] Jim Garamone, "F-22 Safely Shoots Down Chinese Spy Balloon off South Carolina Coast," DOD News, February 4, 2023.

[2] U.S. Senate Committee on Appropriations, "The People's Republic of China's High Altitude Surveillance Efforts Against the United States," video, February 9, 2023.

[3] Federal Aviation Administration (FAA), "Facts About the FAA and Air Traffic Control," February 4, 2020.

[4] We note that some have claimed that there is skepticism within the U.S. government surrounding reports of UAPs. For example, see Bill Whitaker, "UFOs Regularly Spotted in Restricted U.S. Airspace," *CBS News*, August 29, 2021.

[5] James Doubek, "Secret Pentagon Program Spent Millions to Research UFOs," NPR, December 17, 2017.

National Intelligence issued a paper on reports of these objects.[6] In 2022, DoD expanded the Airborne Object Identification and Management Group to the new All-Domain Anomaly Resolution Office.[7] Furthermore, Congress has held hearings on the topic of UAPs.[8]

There are various explanations for these reported UAPs.[9] Some could be consumer drones, U.S. military or civilian aircraft, weather balloons, or merely visual anomalies. Other UAPs could be objects from other countries, including surveillance aircraft or rockets. Finally, some have hypothesized that these objects are extraterrestrial in nature. It was beyond the scope of this research to confirm the sources of public reports of UAPs.

## Democratization of Air Power

The United States has vast amounts of airspace, and a major element of U.S. military doctrine is *air supremacy*, defined as "that degree of control of the air wherein the opposing force is incapable of effective interference within the operational area using air and missile threats."[10] U.S. military leaders have relied on air supremacy to conduct diverse air and space operations around the world, varying from position, navigation, and timing and special operations to power projection and full-on conflict. These operations require a variety of expensive, advanced air and space weapon systems and platforms, including tankers, cargo planes, fighter jets, bombers, remotely piloted aircraft, and sensors. U.S. air and space dominance has largely been unchallenged over the past several decades, due in large part to U.S. prioritization of financial and technological investments in airpower capabilities.

However, although advanced, costly technologies have long been an indicator of airpower and air supremacy, *democratized air power*—increased access to related technologies by interested nation-states, commercial companies, and civilians—may transform this landscape.[11] Drones are becoming increasingly smaller, and commercial air- and spacecraft are becoming much cheaper and easier to access; for example, commercial drones can easily be purchased online or in stores, and one study showed that some small, commercial, unmanned aerial systems are capable of conducting surveillance and reconnaissance, kinetic attacks, or even

---

[6] Office of the Director of National Intelligence, *Preliminary Assessment: Unidentified Aerial Phenomena*, June 25, 2021.

[7] Kathleen Hicks, "Establishment of the All-Domain Anomaly Resolution Office," memorandum for senior Pentagon leadership, commanders of the combatant commands, defense agency and DoD field activity directors, Deputy Secretary of Defense, July 15, 2022.

[8] C-SPAN, "Hearing on Government Investigation of UFOs," video, May 17, 2022.

[9] George Kocher, *UFOs: What to Do?* RAND Corporation, DRU-1571, 1968.

[10] Air University, *Doctrine Advisory: Control of the Air*, U.S. Air Force, July 2017, p. 1.

[11] We note that access to these relevant technologies (e.g., commercially available drones or broadband internet access) is not uniform across the United States.

chemical, biological, or radiological attacks.[12] The commercial space industry is growing in both capacity and capability, and satellite launch costs have decreased dramatically, resulting in exponentially more satellite launches by commercial companies.[13] This has set the stage for how commercial space companies participate in wartime conflicts; a recent example was when Starlink provided internet and imagery capabilities to Ukraine in 2022 during its war with Russia.[14]

The democratization of airpower has been and will likely continue to be enabled by ordinary civilians. At the beginning of the Russia–Ukraine conflict in 2022, Ukraine's military asked Kyiv citizens to donate hobby drones to the warfighting effort.[15] There were crowdfunding efforts to send donations to Ukraine to purchase military equipment, including fighter aircraft and drones. Lithuanian citizens raised 5 million euros to purchase a capable drone for Ukraine, the Bayraktar TB2, developed by the Turkish company Baykar Tech, although the company ended up donating the TB2 to Ukraine's war effort.[16] Other airpower enablers include open-source intelligence, such as that gathered by amateur space observers or by hobbyists who launch balloons equipped with Global Positioning System trackers and cameras into the sky.[17] It is possible that civilians with an interest in observing and examining air and space phenomena could contribute to military situational awareness.[18]

Given recent trends in dual-use technologies (i.e., technologies that can be used for both commercial and military applications), there have been many policy, strategic, and legal questions about the threats posed by their use and development.[19] Nevertheless, civilian and private air and space technologies, employed in addition to purpose-built military weapon

---

[12] Bradley Wilson, Shane Tierney, Brendan Toland, Rachel M. Burns, Colby P. Steiner, Christopher Scott Adams, Michael Nixon, Raza Khan, Michelle D. Ziegler, Jan Osburg, and Ike Chang, *Small Unmanned Aerial System Adversary Capabilities*, RAND Corporation, RR-3023-DHS, 2020.

[13] Emmi Yonekura, Brian Dolan, Moon Kim, Krista Romita Grocholski, Raza Khan, and Yool Kim, *Commercial Space Capabilities and Market Overview: The Relationship Between Commercial Space Developments and the U.S. Department of Defense*, RAND Corporation, RR-A578-2, 2022; Denise Chow, "To Cheaply Go: How Falling Launch Costs Fueled a Thriving Economy in Orbit," NBC News, April 8, 2022.

[14] Julia Siegel, "Commercial Satellites Are on the Front Lines of War Today. Here's What This Means for the Future of Warfare," Atlantic Council, August 30, 2022.

[15] Matt Novak, "Ukraine Military Calls on Citizens with Hobby Drones to Help Kyiv," Gizmodo, February 25, 2022.

[16] Andrius Sytas, "Turkey's Baykar Donates Drone for Ukraine After Lithuanian Crowdfunder," Reuters, June 2, 2022.

[17] Leonard David, "How Amateur Satellite Trackers Are Keeping an 'Eye' on Objects Around the Earth," Space.com, May 3, 2020; Pranshu Verma, "Security Threat or Hot Air? A Guide to High-Altitude Balloons," *Washington Post*, February 16, 2023.

[18] David, 2020.

[19] Linda Slapakova, Theodora Vassilika Ogden, and James Black, "Strategic and Legal Implications of Emerging Dual-Use ASAT Systems," *NATO Legal Gazette*, No. 42, December 2021.

systems, will likely continue to be important factors in future conflicts. This increase in accessibility and operationalization means that understanding UAP reporting trends is a crucial part of mission situational awareness and air supremacy.

## Recent Analyses of Unidentified Aerial Phenomena

Most analyses of UAP reports by the U.S. government have focused on reporting through official channels, including the U.S. Navy and the U.S. Air Force.[20] In contrast, we focused on public reports to a nongovernmental entity, the National UFO Reporting Center (NUFORC). The FAA lists NUFORC as one example of a reporting data collection center in official publications.[21]

We used NUFORC data as a starting point to examine the geographic distribution of UAP reports. Reporting of UAP sightings follows a three-step approach: (1) A person witnesses unexplained activity (usually, but not always) in the sky, (2) the witness reports what they observed to NUFORC, and (3) NUFORC reviews the report for obvious hoaxes before entering the sighting into its database.[22] Our analyses of these data should not be interpreted as an endorsement of any individual reports to NUFORC or of the accuracy of the database. This research serves as a starting point to understand where reported UAP sightings occur and potential associations between the locations of reported sightings and the locations of facilities with known airspace activity, such as military installations and airports.

To this end, we used the available data from NUFORC to answer two questions:

1. Where are people likely to report sightings of UAPs in the United States?
2. What factors predict where people are more or less likely to report UAP sightings?

The remainder of this report outlines our research methods, presents results from our geographic analysis, and concludes with recommendations. We find that the most consistent and statistically significant correlate of public reports of UAPs is being located 30 km or less from military operations areas (MOAs). Thus, we suspect that some public reports of UAPs may in fact be U.S. aircraft flying within MOAs. To ensure accurate reporting of future UAPs of interest to the U.S. government, we recommend that government agencies conduct additional outreach to populations located near MOAs to ensure that the public understands the purpose of this airspace and the types of activities that may be occurring to help reduce the risk of reports of authorized aircraft as UAPs or airborne threats. Furthermore, we recommend an evaluation to inform the design of a detailed and robust system for public reporting of UAP sightings.

---

[20] Office of the Director of National Intelligence, *2022 Annual Report on Unidentified Aerial Phenomena*, January 12, 2023.

[21] FAA, "Air Traffic Plans and Publications," webpage, last modified April 20, 2023b.

[22] We note that NUFORC data include reports of objects inside structures (e.g., homes, hotel rooms).

# CHAPTER 2

# Data and Methods

We obtained data on reported UAP sightings for all 50 U.S. states and Washington, D.C., by web scraping the NUFORC database.[1] NUFORC provides guidance for filing a report, including common phenomena not to report (e.g., planets, Starlink satellites), and it has moderators who appear to review reports before posting them to the public database.[2] We used the data as is and made no additional assumptions about the legitimacy or accuracy of reported sightings.

NUFORC's publicly available data for each sighting include the date of the reported sighting and when the report itself was posted, the location of the sighting (usually a city name), and a description of the sighting. There is no limit on the amount of time that may elapse between when a person witnesses unexplained activity and when a person files a NUFORC report; although active reporting in the public database began in 1998, some reports reference sightings that date back to the early 1900s. We excluded sightings from years prior to active database reporting (1998) to help ensure that our analyses were detecting areas with higher rates of UAP reports relative to the population as a whole rather than one or two retroactive reports from prior years without similar baseline levels of reporting.

We geocoded sightings by city name in ArcGIS StreetMap Premium 2017. We linked geocoded cities to U.S. Census Bureau census designated places (CDPs) by performing a spatial join between the geocoded sightings and the 2010 U.S. Census Bureau CDP shapefile.[3] We obtained decennial total population estimates from 1990 to 2020 in 2010 CDPs from the IPUMS National Historical Geographic Information System.[4] We used linear interpolation

---

[1]  NUFORC, "The National UFO Reporting Center Online Database," webpage, undated-b.

[2]  Reports can be filed directly at NUFORC, "File a Report," webpage, undated-a. The reporting guidance is presented before a person proceeds to the actual reporting form. Contact information for reporters is collected but does not appear in the public database; it is unclear whether reports are routinely followed up on, although some UAP sighting descriptions contain notes on possible explanations from NUFORC, which suggests that some reports are reviewed prior to posting.

[3]  CDPs are the best administrative geographic approximation to cities and towns. We downloaded the CDP shapefile from U.S. Census Bureau, "Mapping Files," webpage, undated.

[4]  Steven Manson, Jonathan Schroeder, David Van Riper, Tracy Kugler, and Steven Ruggles, "IPUMS National Historical Geographic Information System: Version 17.0," dataset, IPUMS, 2022.

to create annual population estimates between decennial years. We calculated CDP population density by dividing estimated total population by land area.

We aggregated UAP sightings annually within CDPs from 1998 to 2022. There were 29,261 2010 CDPs in the United States, which yielded 731,525 CDP-year observations from 1998 to 2022. CDP years with no reported UAPs were assigned a count of 0 sightings. We dropped 410 CDP years with zero total population (observed or interpolated counts). Our final spatial scan statistics and regression analyses included 731,115 CDP years.

To examine whether UAP sightings were more likely to be reported near military installations, we scraped installation names, locations, and branch information from DoD.[5] We obtained latitude and longitude coordinates for installations from the Google Maps link included on each installation's webpage. There was no information on what type of location the coordinates represented (e.g., installation centroid, entrance point, administrative office) or the size of the installation.[6] We performed a spatial join between these points and installation boundaries contained in the U.S. Military Installation National Shapefile.[7] We used the Near (Analysis) tool in ArcMap 10.8.2 to calculate the distance (in kilometers) to the boundary of the nearest installation for each CDP centroid for all installations and by service branch.[8] If a CDP was located within an installation, the distance to the nearest installation was 0.

We obtained data on locations (latitude and longitude) of civilian and military airports and special-use airspace (SUA) from the FAA's master airport record file and airport spatial datasets.[9] We separated civilian and military airports (by branch of service) using name and ownership information. We merged the airport data with the FAA's runway spatial dataset, which allowed us to restrict our analyses to large (one or more runways of at least 7,000 ft) and midsize (one or more runways of 5,000–7,000 ft) civilian airports. We calculated the distance (in kilometers) between CDP centroids and airports using the geonear package in Stata 17.0. We did not include smaller airports, as the vast majority (98 to 99 percent) of CDPs are within a short distance of airports with runways of 5,000 ft or less. The FAA designates several types of SUA; we examined only MOAs because these are the SUAs in which

---

[5]  The U.S. Space Force was established in 2019, resulting in some U.S. Air Force bases becoming Space Force bases. The latter were called Air Force bases for the majority of the period that we are analyzing (1998 to 2022). For this reason, our analysis categorized the six Space Force bases in our dataset as Air Force bases. Military OneSource, "Military Installations," webpage, undated.

[6]  For large installations, the location represented by the coordinates (e.g., installation centroid versus entrance) may substantially shift the distance between the installation and surrounding CDPs.

[7]  U.S. Census Bureau, "TIGER/Line Shapefile, 2019, nation, U.S., Military Installation National Shapefile," data files, January 15, 2021.

[8]  All distance calculations are "as the crow flies," which represents the shortest linear distance between two points.

[9]  FAA, "ADIP: Advanced Facility Search," database, undated-a; ArcGIS Hub, "FAA—Airports," dataset, updated August 6, 2019; FAA, "Runway," dataset, updated April 20, 2023c; FAA, "Special Use Airspace," dataset, updated April 20, 2023d.

military aircraft activity is most likely to be concentrated.[10] MOAs are not always active.[11] However, to our knowledge, there is no publicly accessible historical database of active MOA restrictions, so we used the MOAs identified in the static FAA SUA spatial dataset. We calculated the distance to the nearest civilian airport (by size), military installation (by branch), and MOA for each CDP.[12]

Finally, to account for the possibility that reported UAP sightings may be attributable to weather balloons or weather-related events, we obtained weather station data from the National Oceanic and Atmospheric Administration (NOAA). We used Integrated Global Radiosonde Archive (IGRA) data to find locations (latitude and longitude) of weather stations with radiosonde and pilot balloon observations.[13] We calculated the distance between each CDP centroid and the nearest station annually using geonear to account for changes in activity at these stations across years, and we used NOAA comparative climatic data to measure annual average cloud cover.[14] We assigned each CDP the average percentage of cloudy days using the nearest weather station with available data. Further details about the data cleaning and linkage are provided in the appendix.

We used Kulldorff spatial scan statistics to detect spatial clustering in reported UAP sightings.[15] This method compared the observed distribution of sightings with 999 simulated distributions of sightings randomly generated according to a Poisson process. We used CDP total population as the exposure, which detects clusters of CDPs with higher rates of UAP sightings per population.[16] To do this, the program iteratively drew nonoverlapping circular windows of varying sizes, up to 60 km in radius, around CDPs in both the observed and sim-

---

[10] We thank Josh Becker, Jon Fujiwara, and John Hoehn for lending their expertise in military-relevant topic areas and FAA SUA types and likely activities. We considered including Warning (also known as Whiskey) Airspace in our analyses; however, this SUA extends from three nautical miles off the coast, rendering fewer observations to the public reporting of UAPs in U.S. cities.

[11] Active SUA restrictions can be viewed at FAA, "FAA SUA—Federal Aviation Administration," webpage, undated-b.

[12] As with military installations, distance to a MOA is calculated from the CDP centroid to the nearest point in the MOA boundary. CDPs located inside a MOA have a distance of 0 km.

[13] National Centers for Environmental Information, "Data Access," webpage, undated-b; Integrated Global Radiosonde Archive, "Station Inventory," database, version 2.2, National Centers for Environmental Information, updated January 24, 2023.

[14] National Centers for Environmental Information, "Comparative Climatic Data (CCD)," webpage, undated-a.

[15] Martin Kulldorff, "Spatial Scan Statistics: Models, Calculations, and Applications," in Joseph Glaz and N. Balakrishnan, eds., Scan Statistics and Applications, Birkhäuser, 1999. This method was developed for, and continues to be most commonly used in, spatial epidemiology (e.g., detection of disease clusters).

[16] Setting population as the exposure in a Poisson or a negative binomial model produces results in terms of rates of event counts (in this case, UAP sightings) per population rather than just raw event counts. Using counts of UAP sightings without adjusting for total population produces maps detecting population density rather than areas of increased UAP activity because more people in an area provide more opportunities for UAP reports, even if phenomena perceived to be UAPs occur completely at random across the United States.

ulated datasets to maximize the relative risk of reported UAP sightings inside these windows. We chose 60 km as the maximum cluster radius to approximate the visual horizon distance, but we used alternative maximum radii in our robustness tests.[17] To preserve temporal correlation, sightings had to occur within one to six months of each other to be included in the same cluster. The program uses Monte Carlo hypothesis testing to calculate the statistical significance of the resulting clusters by comparing the likelihood ratios for sightings in observed and simulated datasets. These tests consider the rank of the likelihood ratios for the detected clusters along with the 999 replications simulated under the null hypothesis, which adjusts $p$-values for the testing of multiple hypothesized cluster sizes and locations.[18] We ran the spatial analysis separately for each calendar year to allow detection of repeated clusters of sightings in the same geographic areas. Clusters of UAP sightings were included in our analyses only if the increased relative risk of sightings was statistically significant ($\alpha < 0.05$). We combined results across years in the regression analyses (the analyses included random effects to account for correlations in numbers of UAP sightings in the same CDP across years).

We fit longitudinal negative binomial regression models with random effects at the CDP level to estimate associations between the number of UAP sightings and proximity to military installations, airports, MOAs, and weather stations. We preferred negative binomial models to Poisson models to account for the overdispersion in the number of UAP sightings; most CDPs had no annual reported UAP sightings, although a small number had many. We fit these models with two outcome measures: (1) the total annual number of UAP sightings in CDPs and (2) the annual number of UAP sightings in statistically significant clusters in CDPs. As with the spatial scan analyses, we used the total population as the exposure in both models. This produced results in terms of rates of UAP sightings per population rather than raw counts of sightings.[19] We included random effects at the CDP level to account for correlation among the number of UAP sightings in the same CDPs across years. We controlled for the average annual percentage of cloudy days (which may affect the clarity of objects in the sky) and population density. We also included a set of indicator variables for years, which helped us account for exogenous variation in the frequency of sightings over time. We conducted several robustness checks using alternative model specifications and covariate operationalizations, which we discuss in more detail in the appendix.

Across analyses, our primary geographical unit is CDPs, which vary in size. CDPs are our preferred units of geography because of how UAP locations were reported (by city and state) and the need for a census areal unit to control for estimated population. Some CDPs

---

[17] Specifically, 60 km (approximately 40 miles) is the typical range of very high frequency radio waves, which are approximately bounded by the visual horizon. See National Weather Service, "NOAA Weather Radio Reception," webpage, undated, for more information.

[18] Martin Kulldorff, Farzad Mostashari, Luiz Duczmal, Katherine Yih, Ken Kleinman, and Richard Platt, "Multivariate Scan Statistics for Disease Surveillance," *Statistics in Medicine*, Vol. 26, No. 8, April 2007.

[19] The actual mechanics of using total population as the exposure consist of logging total population into the model as a covariate with the coefficient constrained to be 1.

are very small (less than 1 km), while others are very large (the Sitka, Alaska, CDP has an area of more than 7,000 km). The median CDP land area was 4.7 km² in 2010, with 75 percent of CDPs having land areas of 12.7 km² or less and 95 percent having land areas of less than 60 km², indicating that the majority of CDPs were well within the radii used in the UAP cluster detection and regression analyses. For larger CDPs, there was greater potential discrepancy in where the UAP was sighted compared with the centroid point of the CDP, which is a limitation of the level of geographical specificity of these data. We had no information to assess sightings in smaller areal units (e.g., the U.S. Census Bureau's Zip Code Tabulation Areas), and the use of larger areal units (e.g., counties) would have introduced greater potential discrepancies between sighting and covariate locations.[20]

---

[20] For comparison, the median county land area in 2010 was 1,594.4 km², orders of magnitude larger than CDPs. Furthermore, none of the covariates used in the analyses were measured at the county level. Although there is certainly measurement error associated with locating UAP sightings by CDP centroid (and more so for very large CDPs), aggregating data at the county level may help colocate sightings and covariates that are actually separated by distances much greater than the approximate visual horizon.

# CHAPTER 3

# Results

There were 101,151 reported UAP sightings in 12,783 CDPs from 1998 to 2022. Figure 3.1 shows the distribution of these sightings across years. The number of reported sightings increased from 1998 to 2014, rising particularly sharply in the 2012–2014 period. Sightings then decreased from 2015 to 2018, but they rose again in 2019 and 2020 before returning to approximately 2018 levels in 2021. Overall, an average of 1.76 sightings were reported per 100,000 population each year (see Table A.1 in the appendix for the data underlying Figure 3.1).

**FIGURE 3.1**
**Reported UAP Sightings by Year, 1998–2022**

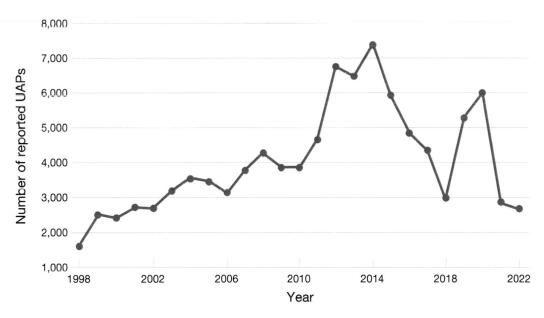

SOURCE: Features data from NUFORC.
NOTE: The years reflect the dates that UAPs were observed, not necessarily the years in which the reports of the sightings were filed.

## Geographic Distribution of Unidentified Aerial Phenomenon Sightings

We identified 751 statistically significant clusters of UAP sightings during this period. The number of clusters detected across years follows a similar pattern as the UAP sightings, except that the total number of clusters peaked in 2013 and 2019 (see Figure A.1 in the appendix). These were both years with higher-than-average numbers of sightings, and the peaks in sighting clusters would better represent when the number of potentially related sightings (i.e., proximity in time and space) was greatest. On average, clusters contained 14.2 UAP sightings. While some clusters were small (two to four sightings), others included more than 100 sightings (see Table A.2 in the appendix).

Figure 3.2 shows the locations of statistically significant clusters of UAP sightings across the United States from 1998 to 2022. Some of the most persistent clusters of sightings were along the coasts of the states of Washington and Oregon, although clusters were found in many areas, including along the East Coast and in rural areas. Figure 3.2 also shows the locations of the military installations and the MOAs.[1] Although some of the UAP clusters appeared near these landmarks on the map, we used regression analyses to test whether spatial proximity of CDPs to these locations increased the likelihood of reporting UAPs that were part of statistically significant clusters of sightings. Table A.3 in the appendix presents descriptive statistics of the variables included in our regression analyses.

## Modeling Unidentified Aerial Phenomenon Sightings

We present results using two dependent outcomes: (1) the total number of annual UAP sightings in CDPs and (2) the annual number of reported UAPs that appeared in a statistically significant cluster of sightings. The first outcome represents the total volume of reported UAPs and is unaffected by the parameters (e.g., the maximum radius size) or results of our spatial scan analyses. The second outcome better reflects associations between covariates and the UAP clusters that our spatial scan statistics identified as being proximate in space and time; however, our significance tests of the associations did not reflect the statistical uncertainty in the identification of the clusters themselves.

The associations between distance to nearest military installation and number of UAPs (both total number and number within significant clusters) are not consistent across distance or branch of service (Table 3.1). Being located near to (30 km or less) or far from (more than 60 km from) U.S. Air Force and U.S. Navy installations was associated with predicted decreases in UAP sightings per total population, as compared with being located within 30 to

---

[1] Locations of IGRA weather stations and civilian airports are shown in Figure A.2 in the appendix. The covariates are displayed in separate figures to increase map legibility.

**FIGURE 3.2**

**Locations of UAP Sighting Clusters, Military Installations, and MOAs, 1998–2022**

SOURCES: Presents data from NUFORC; Military OreScurce, "Military Installations," webpage, undated; FAA, "Special Use Airspace," dataset, updated April 20, 2023d.

NOTE: IGRA weather stations and civilian airports are included in the analyses but not shown on the map because the number of points reduces map legibility. See Figure A.2 in the appendix for these locations. This analysis categorized six Space Force bases in our dataset as Air Force bases.

TABLE 3.1

## Associations Between UAP Sightings and Military Installations, MOAs, and Weather Stations

| | | (1) *N*(All UAPs) | | (2) *N*(UAPs in Clusters) | |
|---|---|---|---|---|---|
| Nearest Military Installation | | IRR | SE | IRR | SE |
| | 30 km or less | 0.837*** | 0.038 | 0.594*** | 0.059 |
| | 30.1 km–60 km | (reference) | | (reference) | |
| Air Force | 60.1 km–120 km | 0.998 | 0.035 | 1.089 | 0.085 |
| | 120.1 km–240 km | 1.011 | 0.035 | 0.908 | 0.072 |
| | More than 240 km | 0.887** | 0.034 | 0.419*** | 0.038 |
| | 30 km or less | 0.786*** | 0.036 | 0.540*** | 0.065 |
| | 30.1 km–60 km | (reference) | | (reference) | |
| Army | 60.1 km–120 km | 1.048 | 0.039 | 1.688*** | 0.147 |
| | 120.1 km–240 km | 0.937 | 0.033 | 1.700*** | 0.145 |
| | More than 240 km | 0.976 | 0.037 | 1.363** | 0.130 |
| | 30 km or less | 0.881 | 0.081 | 1.611* | 0.369 |
| | 30.1 km–60 km | (reference) | | (reference) | |
| Marine Corps | 60.1 km–120 km | 1.275** | 0.103 | 2.481*** | 0.524 |
| | 120.1 km–240 km | 1.170* | 0.086 | 3.271*** | 0.630 |
| | More than 240 km | 1.006 | 0.071 | 1.580* | 0.296 |
| | 30 km or less | 0.858** | 0.041 | 0.734*** | 0.068 |
| | 30.1 km–60 km | (reference) | | (reference) | |
| Navy | 60.1 km–120 km | 0.890** | 0.036 | 0.820* | 0.068 |
| | 120.1 km–240 km | 0.960 | 0.038 | 0.666*** | 0.056 |
| | More than 240 km | 1.044 | 0.040 | 0.550*** | 0.046 |
| Nearest Relevant Location | | | | | |
| | 30 km or less | 1.204*** | 0.035 | 1.486*** | 0.098 |
| | 30.1 km–60 km | (reference) | | (reference) | |
| Nearest MOA | 60.1 km–120 km | 0.976 | 0.026 | 0.790*** | 0.049 |
| | 120.1 km–240 km | 0.975 | 0.028 | 0.862* | 0.059 |
| | More than 240 km | 1.003 | 0.049 | 0.519*** | 0.074 |

## Table 3.1—Continued

| Nearest Relevant Location | | (1) N(All UAPs) | | (2) N(UAPs in Clusters) | |
|---|---|---|---|---|---|
| | | IRR | SE | IRR | SE |
| | 30 km or less | 0.872*** | 0.034 | 0.778** | 0.070 |
| | 30.1 km–60 km | (reference) | | (reference) | |
| Nearest IGRA weather station | 60.1 km–120 km | 0.979 | 0.029 | 0.827** | 0.060 |
| | 120.1 km–240 km | 0.960 | 0.028 | 0.852* | 0.061 |
| | More than 240 km | 1.039 | 0.054 | 0.730* | 0.107 |
| Large civilian airport within 60 km? (1 = Yes) | | 0.831*** | 0.018 | 0.885* | 0.049 |
| Midsize civilian airport within 60 km? (1 = Yes) | | 0.821*** | 0.027 | 0.767** | 0.065 |
| Percentage of cloudy days | | 1.016*** | 0.001 | 1.088*** | 0.003 |
| Population density (logged) | | 0.772*** | 0.006 | 0.616*** | 0.013 |
| Constant | | 0.000*** | 0.000 | 0.000*** | 0.000 |

NOTE: IRR = incident rate ratio; SE = standard error. Results were obtained from multivariate negative binomial regression models. $N = 731{,}115$. Indicator variables for years are included but not shown. Total population is included as the model exposure; its coefficient is constrained to be 1 and not shown in the table. IRRs compare rates among two different groups; an IRR of 1 is parity, an IRR < 1 indicates predicted decreases in rates, and an IRR > 1 indicates predicted increases in rates. * $p < 0.05$, ** $p < 0.01$, *** $p < 0.001$. This analysis categorized six Space Force bases in our dataset as Air Force bases.

60 km of an installation.[2] This result was not generated by the choice of 60 km as the maximum possible radius for UAP clusters, given that these findings were consistent when we used the total number of UAP sightings as the outcome (column 1 of Table 3.1). Using one measure for all military installations (Table A.5 in the appendix), examining the locations of military installations (Table A.6), and omitting MOAs (Table A.7) did not substantively alter these findings.

Alternatively, being located near a MOA was associated with predicted increases in the rate of UAP sightings. For all UAP sightings, we estimated that the rate of reports within 30 km of a MOA was 1.20 times greater than the rate within 30.1 km to 60 km of a MOA, other covariates in the model being equal. For UAP sightings in clusters, we estimated that the rate was 1.49 times higher when the CDP was located within 30 km of a MOA than when located within 30.1 km to 60 km. Additionally, for UAP sightings in clusters, being located farther from a MOA (60.1 km to 120 km, 120.1 km to 240 km, and more than 240 km) was

---

[2] To alleviate concerns about collinearity among covariates (e.g., distance to Air Force installations and MOAs may both be capturing proximity to areal military activity), we estimated a series of models that included each covariate of interest individually rather than fully adjusted for all covariates (see Table A.4 in the appendix). Associations were similar to those presented in the full multivariate models in Table 3.1, suggesting that collinearity between covariates is not producing these results.

associated with expected reductions in the rate of sightings, as compared with being within 30.1 km to 60 km of a MOA, other covariates being equal.

Being located within 60 km of a large or midsize civilian airport was associated with reduced rates of UAP sightings. For all UAPs, our models showed that being located within 60 km of a large civilian airport decreased the rate of UAP sightings by a factor of 0.83, other covariates being equal. The associations were similar for UAP sightings in clusters and for midsize civilian airports.

Distance to the nearest IGRA weather station did not reflect consistent associations with UAP sightings. For all UAP sightings and UAP sightings in clusters, being located within 30 km of a weather station, as compared with 30.1 km–60 km, was expected to decrease the rate of sightings; however, for UAP sightings in clusters, being located farther than 60 km also appeared to decrease the rate of sightings, other covariates being equal, as compared with being within 30.1 km to 60 km. The percentage of cloudy days was positively associated with expected UAP sightings, such that for each additional 1 percent of cloudy days, the expected rate of all UAP sightings increased by 1.6 percent, other covariates being equal.

We were concerned that these results could have been generated by the persistent clustering of UAP sightings along the coastlines of the states of Washington and Oregon, but the associations were not substantively altered when we omitted these states from the analysis (see Table A.8 in the appendix). Finally, population density was negatively associated with UAP sightings, suggesting that rural areas have a higher rate of expected UAP reports, other covariates being equal.

## Model Robustness Checks

We performed several robustness checks on these results. First, we used alternative maximum cluster radii to determine whether the choice of 60 km for the maximum cluster radius substantively affected our results. UAP sighting clusters are located in similar areas when using 50-km and 100-km radii (Figure A.3 in the appendix), and the results were consistent with those for 60-km maximum radius clusters (Table A.9). Second, because many CDPs have zero UAP sightings each year, we also fit a multivariate logistic regression with a binary outcome for whether a CDP year had any reported UAP sightings (1 = Yes); the results were consistent with the negative binomial models for number of UAP sightings (Table A.10, column 1). Third, we selected a counterfactual set of CDPs with similar population sizes to those with observed UAP reports. The analysis of these CDPs produced largely null results and entirely null results for distance to the nearest MOA, suggesting that our findings were not merely reflecting the general proximity of CDPs to MOAs. (Results from a logistic regression model using a binary outcome for whether a CDP year had any reported UAP sightings [1 = Yes] are shown in Table A.10, column 2, and results from a negative binomial model are shown in Table A.11.)

## Limitations

Our analyses have several limitations. First, we had limited information and insights into how NUFORC collects data. It is possible that clusters of reports refer to the same UAP sighted by different individuals, multiple reports by the same individual, or reports that are not UAPs. Furthermore, we had limited insights into how NUFORC adjudicates what is or is not a legitimate UAP sighting. Historically, there has been distrust between amateur researchers of UAPs and government officials tasked with studying these phenomena.[3]

Second, we did not account for the statistical uncertainty of cluster detection in our regression models that used sightings in clusters as an outcome variable; however, we estimated several alternative models to check the robustness of our findings. It should also be noted that the spatial scan statistics specifically detected *circular* areas with higher rates of UAP reports per population. Our estimation of similar associations for all reported UAPs, not just those contained in statistically significant clusters, should reduce concerns that cluster shape is primarily driving our results, but we acknowledge that areas with higher rates of UAP sightings could manifest in various irregular shapes.

Third, NUFORC is located in Davenport, Washington, and the persistent clusters of UAP sightings in Washington could be generated in part by increased awareness of NUFORC's data collection efforts among those living in the state. Omitting sightings from Washington did not substantively alter associations between covariates and the likelihood of UAP sightings in the regression models, indicating that our findings are not driven by these clusters.

Finally, our results are associational, not causal. We make no causal claims about the relationships between variables in our models (e.g., reports near MOAs), but we note that there was a robust and statistically significant relationship for UAP reports within 30 km of MOAs in NUFORC's dataset.

---

[3] Greg Eghigian, "Making UFOs Make Sense: Ufology, Science, and the History of Their Mutual Mistrust," *Public Understanding of Science*, Vol. 26, No. 5, July 2017.

# CHAPTER 4

# Conclusions and Recommendations

The U.S. Air Force's downing of a Chinese surveillance balloon that flew across the country in early 2023 raised concerns about the degree to which the U.S. government knows who is flying what across its vast airspace. Like most countries, the United States has finite resources to monitor its skies. Technological advances are making it cheaper and easier for civilians, private companies, civilian government agencies, and foreign actors to access and deploy ever-smaller aerial devices (e.g., drones, surveillance balloons). Given these trends, public reporting of aerial phenomena could be an asset for government authorities to identify potential threats in U.S. airspace.

As a starting point to assess the utility of this information, should U.S. government authorities wish to leverage public UAP reporting channels, we examined where people are claiming they have seen these phenomena. We analyzed data on 101,151 reported UAP sightings from 12,783 CDPs from 1998 to 2022 from the NUFORC database. Note that our analyses do not imply an endorsement of any individual reports of UAPs or the accuracy of the overall database. Furthermore, our models included a limited number of covariates, and there is a need for future research to address other potential explanatory factors using the models presented in this report.

Our statistical models predicted two outcomes of interest: the total number of UAPs over time and the total number of UAPs in clusters that accounted for a significantly higher number of reports relative to the rest of the country. Both of these models found inconsistent results in the relationship between the nearest military installations and self-reports of UAP sightings. For example, there was a higher likelihood of UAP reports in areas that were within 60.1 km to 120 km of a Marine Corps installation, as compared with 30.1 km to 60 km, but there was some evidence that reports were less likely in areas within 30 km of these same installations.

We found inconsistent results when we examined the association between proximity to weather stations with reported launches of government weather balloons and self-reports of UAP sightings. We also found negative associations in our models for UAP reports within 30 km of weather stations, within 60 km of civilian airports, and in more-densely populated areas. One possible explanation for this pattern of findings is that people located in more-densely populated areas, near airports and near weather stations, are more aware of the types of objects that fly overhead and nearby and are therefore less apt to report aerial phenomena.

The most consistent—and statistically significant—finding from our models was for reports of UAP sightings in areas within 30 km of MOAs. According to the FAA, "MOAs are established to contain nonhazardous, military flight activities," including air combat maneuvers, air intercepts, and low-altitude tactics.[1] Given this association, we suspect that some of the self-reports of UAP sightings to NUFORC are authorized aircraft flying within MOAs. However, it was beyond the scope of this research to confirm the context of these UAP self-reports beyond their documented locations in the NUFORC database.

## Recommendations

The results from this analysis point to three recommendations for government officials. The first two recommendations broadly relate to communications with the public, and the third relates to improvements in data collection.

- First, **we recommend that government authorities (e.g., local and state government officials, the FAA, and DoD) conduct outreach with civilians located near MOAs**. We hypothesize that many civilians may not be aware that they are located near areas where military operations occur. If our results are correct—that is, if being located within 30 km of a MOA is significantly associated with UAP reports, and if some of these reported objects are in fact authorized aircraft—then communicating that such activities are being conducted nearby could reduce the likelihood that the public will report these aircraft as UAPs.
- Second, **we recommend that government authorities conduct additional outreach to notify nearby civilians when there is airspace activity near a MOA**. According to the FAA, not all MOAs are in use by authorized aircraft.[2] When appropriate, notifying local populations of MOA activities could reduce the number of reported UAPs that are in fact authorized aircraft.
- Finally, **we recommend an evaluation to inform the design of a detailed and robust system for public reporting of UAP sightings**. Such an evaluation would inform the use of various technologies (e.g., mobile devices, artificial intelligence), reports on location types (e.g., street intersections, landmarks, latitude and longitude coordinates), sighting features (e.g., images, audio recordings), criteria for validating these reports, and who is best equipped to independently manage such a reporting system (e.g., government agencies, for-profit companies, nonprofit organizations, international organizations). Such a system would be useful in minimizing hoaxes and reports of misidentified objects.

---

[1]  FAA, "Chapter 25. Military Operations Areas: Section 1. General," *Order JO 7400.2P—Procedures for Handling Airspace Matters*, March 17, 2023a.

[2]  FAA, "Chapter 15: Airspace," *Pilot's Handbook of Aeronautical Knowledge*, August 24, 2016.

In conclusion, the U.S. government has a large swath of airspace to monitor at a time when there is greater access than ever to small, technologically advanced, and inexpensive aerial objects. If officials believe that public reporting could be a valuable tool to help manage U.S. airspace, it will be important to ensure that members of the public report actual threats. Greater transparency in how sightings are collected, investigated, and used may also help mitigate the conspiracy theories that have long surrounded aerial phenomena.

# Methodological Details and Data Preparation

## Reported Unidentified Aerial Phenomenon

We scraped 125,366 UAP sightings from the NUFORC database on November 15, 2022, using Beautiful Soup in Python 2.7. We collected all available database entries for the 50 U.S. states and Washington, D.C., regardless of the completeness of the sighting report or the date of sighting. Information was available for both the approximate date and time the UAP was observed and the date the sighting was reported. For our analyses, we dated sightings by the observation date; we did not impose restrictions on the length of time between the observation and when the report was submitted to NUFORC. Because of a lag in time between some observations and the filing of the report, the majority of 2022 UAP sightings in our data occurred between January and September.

We then prepared the dates and locations of UAP sightings from the raw data to be geocoded.[1] We were able to extract month and year from the raw date and time information for 125,109 UAP sightings (99.8 percent). Location information was most commonly recorded as the city and state in which the UAP was observed. Some form of city name information was available for 124,960 sightings (99.7 percent); 314 sightings had missing or "unknown" location information, and 116 sightings originated from air travel. If more than one city name was reported (e.g., Culver City and Los Angeles, Calif.; State College and Bellefonte, Pa.), we used the first city name in the entry. We geocoded city names using the "AdminPlaces" locator file in ArcGIS StreetMap Premium 2017 in ArcGIS 10.8.2 to obtain latitude and longitude coordinates. We successfully geocoded 97.2 percent of the sightings that were not missing city information ($N$ = 121,438 of 124,960). In total, we were able to date and locate 121,201 of the 125,366 UAP sightings scraped from NUFORC (96.7 percent).

UAP sighting data appear to be generated by a three-step process: (1) Someone witnesses an unknown phenomenon, (2) they submit a report to NUFORC, and (3) NUFORC reviews

---

[1] As noted above, we made no assumptions about the underlying accuracy or credibility of reported sightings in the NUFORC data. The data preparation we describe here was not an attempt to filter observations from (or verify observations in) the NUFORC data but rather an attempt to transform date information contained in text strings into standard formats able to be processed by statistical programs (in this case, Stata 17.0MP and SaTScan v10.1) and to separate location information into fields readable to ArcGIS (e.g., city name, state abbreviation). This is standard practice when preparing administrative data for statistical analysis.

and potentially posts the report to its public database. For our analyses, we were most interested in identifying areas with higher rates of UAP activity, holding the context and likelihood of reporting that activity approximately constant. To do this, we placed two additional restrictions on the UAP sightings included in our analyses.

First, to help account for the risk that larger populations increased the likelihood that one or more individuals witnessed the same unknown activity in the sky and then reported it to NUFORC, we needed to account for population distribution across cities. A map of UAP sightings that does not account for population is likely to merely approximate population density rather than reflect areas of increased UAP activity across the country. To get population estimates for cities, we joined the UAP data to CDPs (the closest approximation to cities in U.S. census data) by performing a spatial join between city latitude and longitude coordinates and the 2010 census CDP shapefile. Cities were only assigned a CDP if their coordinates were within a CDP's boundaries ($N = 111,837$ or 92.3 percent of sightings with valid date and location information).

Not all land area within the United States is included in a CDP; the 7.7 percent of the sightings in our data that were not within a CDP were excluded from the analyses because of the lack of information on total population (an important control in both our spatial scan and regression analyses). Areas not included in CDPs are likely to be in very rural, low-population areas outside official town, city, or borough boundaries. Although it is possible to obtain population estimates for all areas within a state that are not contained in a CDP, we could not include these as separate "areas," as total state land area is substantially larger than CDPs and non-CDP areas occur throughout states. For example, combining population and UAP sightings not contained in CDPs in California into one observation would aggregate reports from rural areas near the Oregon border in the north with those in Imperial County (along the Mexican border) in the south, which would have occurred approximately 1,000 km apart.

Second, UAP sightings can be reported to NUFORC at any time; the earliest reporting dates in the online database were from 1998 but some reports reference sightings that date back to the early 1900s. We restricted our analyses to 1998–2022 to account for a higher probability that the events in our dataset were reported to NUFORC within a relatively short period (e.g., a few days or weeks) and not retroactively by many years. Setting limits on our data decreased the likelihood that we identified "false positive" UAP clusters in, for example, 1968 because of unusually high retrospective reporting rather than actual increased UAP activity in that year. This resulted in 101,151 UAP sightings included in our analyses.

As a robustness check that the results in our regression analyses were not generated by a general propensity of types of CDPs with UAP sightings located near MOAs or other covariates of interest, we generated two counterfactual sample CDPs. In the first, we randomly assigned the same number of UAP sightings within similarly sized CDPs. In the second, we created an indicator for whether at least one UAP sighting was reported in a CDP year. We then randomly selected similarly sized CDPs to those that had at least one sighting included in a UAP cluster each year. We did this by stratifying CDPs into 60 strata by total population annually and randomly selecting $Nb$ CDPs from each strata (b), where $Nb =$ the number of CDPs in strata $b$ that had at least one observed UAP sighting in a statistically significant cluster (maximum radius of 60 km) in that year. For the first counterfactual sample, we fit a negative binomial model with the UAP count as the outcome. For the second counterfactual sample, we fit a multivariate logistic regression model using a binary indicator of whether a CDP year was included in the counterfactual sample (1 = Yes) as the outcome. We constructed the counterfactual sample in two parts because of the difficulty reproducing the (very) skewed distribution of UAP counts across CDPs.

## Military Installations and Military Operations Areas

We scraped location and service branch information for 337 military installations on February 22, 2023. We excluded six installations associated with the Defense Logistics Agency, 42 U.S. Army Recruiting Command (USAREC) installations, and nine U.S. Army Cadet Command installations, which appeared to be primarily focused on Reserve Officers' Training Corps activities. We categorized the six U.S. Space Force bases in our dataset as Air Force bases. We excluded 89 National Guard installations because many were located in or directly adjacent to Army or Air Force installations or airports, which were already included in the analyses. There were an additional ten installations that were not included in the U.S. Military Installation National Shapefile and had to be excluded because of a lack of installation boundary information:

- Air Force (2): Pentagon, U.S. Air Force Academy
- Army (4): Fort McCoy, Camp Parks, U.S. Southern Command/U.S. Army Garrison–Miami, Hunter Army Airfield
- Navy (3): Newport News Shipyard, Stennis Space Center, Surface Combat Systems Center Wallops Island
- Marine Corps (1): Marine Corps Community Services Hampton Roads.

The final dataset contained 181 installations: 63 Air Force, 47 Army, 16 Marine Corps, and 55 Navy. For installations named as a "Joint Base" ($N$ = 12), we collected information on up to three service branches associated with each base. Joint bases were represented once in total installation counts but could appear in more than one service branch type (i.e., a joint installation could be counted as both the nearest Air Force installation and the nearest Army installation).

TABLE A.1

## Rates of UAP Sightings in the United States by Year

| Year | Total CDP Population | Number of Sightings | Sightings per 100,000 Population |
|------|--------------------:|--------------------:|--------------------------------:|
| 1998 | 205,828,095 | 1,593 | 0.77 |
| 1999 | 207,973,145 | 2,504 | 1.20 |
| 2000 | 210,117,690 | 2,416 | 1.15 |
| 2001 | 211,951,977 | 2,717 | 1.28 |
| 2002 | 213,785,519 | 2,679 | 1.25 |
| 2003 | 215,619,910 | 3,200 | 1.48 |
| 2004 | 217,453,386 | 3,551 | 1.63 |
| 2005 | 219,289,867 | 3,459 | 1.58 |
| 2006 | 221,121,437 | 3,132 | 1.42 |
| 2007 | 222,955,890 | 3,759 | 1.69 |
| 2008 | 224,789,351 | 4,289 | 1.91 |
| 2009 | 226,623,791 | 3,858 | 1.70 |
| 2010 | 228,457,238 | 3,864 | 1.69 |
| 2011 | 230,144,055 | 4,655 | 2.02 |
| 2012 | 231,829,435 | 6,758 | 2.92 |
| 2013 | 233,516,320 | 6,478 | 2.77 |
| 2014 | 235,201,759 | 7,381 | 3.14 |
| 2015 | 236,891,550 | 5,920 | 2.50 |
| 2016 | 238,573,793 | 4,844 | 2.03 |
| 2017 | 240,260,737 | 4,337 | 1.81 |
| 2018 | 241,946,052 | 2,975 | 1.23 |
| 2019 | 243,633,004 | 5,263 | 2.16 |
| 2020 | 245,318,333 | 6,010 | 2.45 |
| 2021 | 247,005,325 | 2,834 | 1.15 |
| 2022 | 248,691,677 | 2,675 | 1.08 |
| Average | 227,959,173 | 4,046 | 1.76 |

TABLE A.2

## Statistically Significant Clusters of UAP Sightings by Year

| Year | Number of UAP Clusters | Number of UAP Sightings in Clusters | | | | |
| --- | --- | --- | --- | --- | --- | --- |
| | | Mean | Std. Dev. | Min. | Median | Max. |
| 1998 | 8 | 15.75 | 18.66 | 4.00 | 7.00 | 55.00 |
| 1999 | 26 | 10.88 | 16.16 | 2.00 | 5.00 | 79.00 |
| 2000 | 12 | 19.25 | 23.71 | 2.00 | 6.50 | 72.00 |
| 2001 | 20 | 16.00 | 21.60 | 2.00 | 6.00 | 85.00 |
| 2002 | 19 | 10.32 | 16.10 | 2.00 | 5.00 | 67.00 |
| 2003 | 23 | 12.61 | 18.36 | 2.00 | 7.00 | 86.00 |
| 2004 | 19 | 22.32 | 28.10 | 2.00 | 12.00 | 94.00 |
| 2005 | 27 | 12.63 | 16.50 | 2.00 | 6.00 | 57.00 |
| 2006 | 22 | 9.73 | 10.04 | 3.00 | 6.00 | 47.00 |
| 2007 | 26 | 9.23 | 8.94 | 2.00 | 5.50 | 39.00 |
| 2008 | 32 | 8.28 | 8.21 | 2.00 | 5.00 | 41.00 |
| 2009 | 24 | 7.88 | 8.05 | 2.00 | 5.50 | 41.00 |
| 2010 | 29 | 12.79 | 16.38 | 2.00 | 8.00 | 79.00 |
| 2011 | 35 | 15.00 | 15.64 | 3.00 | 10.00 | 83.00 |
| 2012 | 44 | 16.89 | 16.55 | 2.00 | 13.00 | 83.00 |
| 2013 | 67 | 20.14 | 17.84 | 3.00 | 15.00 | 97.00 |
| 2014 | 37 | 23.57 | 27.65 | 3.00 | 13.00 | 129.00 |
| 2015 | 38 | 19.74 | 16.89 | 3.00 | 13.00 | 78.00 |
| 2016 | 27 | 17.07 | 20.51 | 2.00 | 8.00 | 80.00 |
| 2017 | 23 | 12.35 | 13.38 | 3.00 | 7.00 | 58.00 |
| 2018 | 32 | 8.03 | 5.67 | 2.00 | 6.00 | 27.00 |
| 2019 | 58 | 12.22 | 8.15 | 2.00 | 10.00 | 36.00 |
| 2020 | 56 | 15.30 | 11.91 | 4.00 | 11.00 | 64.00 |
| 2021 | 33 | 8.82 | 7.54 | 2.00 | 7.00 | 37.00 |
| 2022 | 24 | 10.67 | 7.45 | 2.00 | 9.00 | 36.00 |
| Total | 751 | 14.17 | 16.11 | 2.00 | 8.00 | 129.00 |

NOTE: Max. = maximum; Min. = minimum; Std. Dev. = standard deviation. Only statistically significant clusters (a < 0.05) were included in analyses.

TABLE A.3

**Descriptive Statistics for Regression Analyses (CDP Characteristics)**

| Sighting Characteristics | N | Mean | Std. Dev. | Min. | Median | Max. |
|---|---|---|---|---|---|---|
| Number of UAPs | 731,115 | 0.14 | 0.87 | 0.00 | 0.00 | 93.00 |
| Number of UAPs in stat. sig. cluster (60-km max. radius) | 731,115 | 0.01 | 0.33 | 0.00 | 0.00 | 90.00 |
| Total CDP population | 731,115 | 7,794.92 | 66,568.04 | 1.00 | 1,052.00 | 8,930,415.00 |
| Population density | 731,115 | 1,282.87 | 1,863.14 | 0.01 | 758.55 | 92,927.24 |
| Percentage of cloudy days | 731,115 | 43.30 | 8.93 | 14.25 | 43.84 | 83.52 |

NOTE: stat. sig. = statistically significant. The unit of observation (N) for the analysis was CDP years. As there were only 101,151 reported sightings during the period of study, many of those CDP years have zero reported sightings.

TABLE A.4

**Descriptive Statistics for Regression Analyses (Nearest Relevant Location)**

| Nearest Relevant Location | N | % |
|---|---|---|
| Nearest military installation (all) | | |
| 30 km or less | 104,211 | 14.25 |
| 30.1 km–60 km | 121,039 | 16.56 |
| 60.1 km–120 km | 193,672 | 26.49 |
| 120.1 km–240 km | 215,873 | 29.53 |
| More than 240 km | 96,320 | 13.17 |
| | | |
| Nearest Air Force installation | | |
| 30 km or less | 44,071 | 6.03 |
| 30.1 km–60 km | 65,800 | 9.00 |
| 60.1 km–120 km | 156,971 | 21.47 |
| 120.1 km–240 km | 259,111 | 35.44 |
| More than 240 km | 205,162 | 28.06 |

## Table A.4 —Continued

| Nearest Relevant Location | N | % |
|---|---|---|
| Nearest Army installation | | |
| 30 km or less | 47,366 | 6.48 |
| 30.1 km–60 km | 65,272 | 8.93 |
| 60.1 km–120 km | 127,912 | 17.50 |
| 120.1 km–240 km | 264,116 | 36.13 |
| More than 240 km | 226,449 | 30.97 |
| | | |
| Nearest Marine Corps installation | | |
| 30 km or less | 11,425 | 1.56 |
| 30.1 km–60 km | 10,873 | 1.49 |
| 60.1 km–120 km | 27,870 | 3.81 |
| 120.1 km–240 km | 81,617 | 11.16 |
| More than 240 km | 599,330 | 81.97 |
| | | |
| Nearest Navy installation | | |
| 30 km or less | 38,997 | 5.33 |
| 30.1 km–60 km | 44,225 | 6.05 |
| 60.1 km–120 km | 98,626 | 13.49 |
| 120.1 km–240 km | 170,715 | 23.35 |
| More than 240 km | 378,552 | 51.78 |
| | | |
| Nearest MOA | | |
| 30 km or less | 166,969 | 22.84 |
| 30.1 km–60 km | 139,648 | 19.10 |
| 60.1 km–120 km | 226,037 | 30.92 |
| 120.1 km–240 km | 167,535 | 22.91 |
| More than 240 km | 30,926 | 4.23 |

## Table A.4 —Continued

| Nearest Relevant Location | N | % |
|---|---|---|
| Nearest IGRA weather station | | |
| 30 km or less | 42,891 | 5.87 |
| 30.1 km–60 km | 81,845 | 11.19 |
| 60.1 km–120 km | 209,891 | 28.71 |
| 120.1 km–240 km | 361,055 | 49.38 |
| More than 240 km | 35,433 | 4.85 |
| | | |
| Nearest large civilian airport (at least 1 runway ≥ 7,000 ft) | | |
| 30 km or less | 232,851 | 31.85 |
| 30.1 km–60 km | 241,121 | 32.98 |
| 60.1 km–120 km | 218,877 | 29.94 |
| 120.1 km–240 km | 35,688 | 4.88 |
| More than 240 km | 2,578 | 0.35 |
| | | |
| Nearest midsize civilian airport (at least 1 runway ≥ 5,000 ft but less than 7,000 ft) | | |
| 30 km or less | 396,550 | 54.24 |
| 30.1 km–60 km | 257,566 | 35.23 |
| 60.1 km–120 km | 72,341 | 9.89 |
| 120.1 km–240 km | 4,386 | 0.60 |
| More than 240 km | 272 | 0.04 |

NOTE: This analysis categorized six Space Force bases in our dataset as Air Force bases.

TABLE A.5

# Unadjusted Associations Between UAP Sightings and Covariates

| Nearest Military Installation | | (1) N(All UAPs) | | (2) N(UAPs in Clusters) | |
|---|---|---|---|---|---|
| | | IRR | SE | IRR | SE |
| | 30 km or less | 0.718*** | 0.031 | 0.474*** | 0.045 |
| | 30.1 km–60 km | (reference) | | (reference) | |
| Air Force | 60.1 km–120 km | 1.150*** | 0.042 | 1.937*** | 0.151 |
| | 120.1 km–240 km | 1.250*** | 0.043 | 1.955*** | 0.147 |
| | More than 240 km | 1.137*** | 0.040 | 1.004 | 0.083 |
| | 30 km or less | 0.688*** | 0.022 | 0.552*** | 0.061 |
| | 30.1 km–60 km | (reference) | | (reference) | |
| Army | 60.1 km–120 km | 1.160*** | 0.037 | 1.701*** | 0.145 |
| | 120.1 km–240 km | 1.009 | 0.038 | 0.953 | 0.075 |
| | More than 240 km | 1.142*** | 0.052 | 0.729*** | 0.062 |
| | 30 km or less | 0.715** | 0.046 | 1.282 | 0.317 |
| | 30.1 km–60 km | (reference) | | (reference) | |
| Marine Corps | 60.1 km–120 km | 1.470*** | 0.128 | 4.103*** | 0.965 |
| | 120.1 km–240 km | 1.392*** | 0.104 | 7.507*** | 1.573 |
| | More than 240 km | 1.358*** | 0.093 | 4.407*** | 0.885 |
| | 30 km or less | 0.712*** | 0.035 | 0.696*** | 0.067 |
| | 30.1 km–60 km | (reference) | | (reference) | |
| Navy | 60.1 km–120 km | 0.985 | 0.044 | 0.924 | 0.080 |
| | 120.1 km–240 km | 1.161*** | 0.046 | 0.977 | 0.080 |
| | More than 240 km | 1.310*** | 0.050 | 0.548*** | 0.042 |
| **Nearest Relevant Location** | | | | | |
| | 30 km or less | 1.379*** | 0.043 | 1.952*** | 0.129 |
| | 30.1 km–60 km | (reference) | | (reference) | |
| Nearest MOA | 60.1 km–120 km | 0.922** | 0.027 | 0.538*** | 0.034 |
| | 120.1 km–240 km | 0.909** | 0.028 | 0.741*** | 0.050 |
| | More than 240 km | 0.777*** | 0.039 | 0.401*** | 0.056 |

## Table A.5—Continued

| Nearest Relevant Location | | (1) *N*(All UAPs) | | (2) *N*(UAPs in Clusters) | |
|---|---|---|---|---|---|
| | | IRR | SE | IRR | SE |
| Nearest IGRA weather station | 30 km or less | 0.823*** | 0.034 | 0.386*** | 0.037 |
| | 30.1 km–60 km | (reference) | | (reference) | |
| | 60.1 km–120 km | 1.106** | 0.034 | 1.137 | 0.086 |
| | 120.1 km–240 km | 1.147*** | 0.034 | 1.608*** | 0.115 |
| | More than 240 km | 1.357*** | 0.074 | 1.144 | 0.171 |
| Large civilian airport within 60 km? (1 = Yes) | | 0.627*** | 0.013 | 0.418*** | 0.022 |
| Midsize civilian airport within 60 km? (1 = Yes) | | 0.713*** | 0.025 | 0.854 | 0.076 |
| Percentage of cloudy days | | 1.011*** | 0.001 | 1.076*** | 0.002 |
| Population density (logged) | | 0.731*** | 0.006 | 0.590*** | 0.011 |

NOTE: IRR = incident rate ratio; SE = standard error. Results were obtained from separate negative binomial regression models in which each covariate of interest was entered individually, adjusting only for year (indicator variables included but not shown) and total population (as the exposure; its coefficient is constrained to be 1 and not shown in the table). $N$ = 731,115. IRRs compare rates among two different groups; an IRR of 1 is parity, an IRR < 1 indicates predicted decreases in rates, and an IRR > 1 indicates predicted increases in rates. ** $p < 0.01$, *** $p < 0.001$. This analysis categorized six Space Force bases in our dataset as Air Force bases.

TABLE A.6

## Associations Between UAP Sightings and Military Installations, All Service Branches

| Nearest Relevant Location | | (1) *N*(All UAPs) | | (2) *N*(UAPs in Clusters) | |
|---|---|---|---|---|---|
| | | IRR | SE | IRR | SE |
| Nearest military installation (all branches) | 30 km or less | 0.804*** | 0.025 | 0.575*** | 0.039 |
| | 30.1 km–60 km | (reference) | | (reference) | |
| | 60.1 km–120 km | 0.914** | 0.026 | 0.778*** | 0.050 |
| | 120.1 km–240 km | 0.960 | 0.028 | 0.620*** | 0.042 |
| | More than 240 km | 0.952 | 0.035 | 0.338*** | 0.032 |
| Nearest MOA | 30 km or less | 1.201*** | 0.035 | 1.503*** | 0.098 |
| | 30.1 km–60 km | (reference) | | (reference) | |
| | 60.1 km–120 km | 0.976 | 0.026 | 0.753*** | 0.046 |
| | 120.1 km–240 km | 0.979 | 0.028 | 0.876* | 0.057 |
| | More than 240 km | 0.977 | 0.046 | 0.574*** | 0.080 |
| Nearest IGRA weather station | 30 km or less | 0.872*** | 0.034 | 0.698*** | 0.063 |
| | 30.1 km–60 km | (reference) | | (reference) | |
| | 60.1 km–120 km | 1.003 | 0.029 | 0.964 | 0.069 |
| | 120.1 km–240 km | 0.961 | 0.027 | 0.905 | 0.063 |
| | More than 240 km | 1.019 | 0.053 | 0.721* | 0.105 |
| Large civilian airport | | 0.810*** | 0.018 | 0.808*** | 0.045 |
| Midsize civilian airport | | 0.831*** | 0.027 | 0.860 | 0.072 |
| Percentage of cloudy days | | 1.013*** | 0.001 | 1.073*** | 0.002 |
| Population density (logged) | | 0.763*** | 0.006 | 0.617*** | 0.013 |
| Constant | | 0.001*** | 0.000 | 0.000*** | 0.000 |

NOTE: IRR = incident rate ratio; SE = standard error. Results were obtained from multivariate negative binomial regression models. $N = 731{,}115$. Indicator variables for years are included but not shown. Total population is included as the model exposure; its coefficient is constrained to be 1 and not shown in the table. IRRs compare rates among two different groups; an IRR of 1 is parity, an IRR < 1 indicates predicted decreases in rates, and an IRR > 1 indicates predicted increases in rates. * $p < 0.05$, ** $p < 0.01$, *** $p < 0.001$. This analysis categorized six Space Force bases in our dataset as Air Force bases.

TABLE A.7

## Associations Between UAP Sightings and Military Installations

| Nearest Military Installation | | (1) *N*(All UAPs) | | (2) *N*(UAPs in Clusters) | |
|---|---|---|---|---|---|
| | | IRR | SE | IRR | SE |
| Air Force | 30 km or less | 0.761*** | 0.035 | 0.526*** | 0.053 |
| | 30.1 km–60 km | (reference) | | (reference) | |
| | 60.1 km–120 km | 0.971 | 0.033 | 1.159* | 0.087 |
| | 120.1 km–240 km | 0.884*** | 0.030 | 0.843* | 0.065 |
| | More than 240 km | 0.950 | 0.036 | 0.568*** | 0.052 |
| Army | 30 km or less | 0.687*** | 0.030 | 0.478*** | 0.050 |
| | 30.1 km–60 km | (reference) | | (reference) | |
| | 60.1 km–120 km | 1.001 | 0.033 | 1.087 | 0.085 |
| | 120.1 km–240 km | 1.007 | 0.032 | 1.009 | 0.078 |
| | More than 240 km | 1.013 | 0.036 | 0.988 | 0.084 |
| Marine Corps | 30 km or less | 1.038 | 0.154 | 0.466* | 0.146 |
| | 30.1 km–60 km | (reference) | | (reference) | |
| | 60.1 km–120 km | 1.109 | 0.123 | 1.141 | 0.258 |
| | 120.1 km–240 km | 0.970 | 0.101 | 0.414*** | 0.091 |
| | More than 240 km | 0.843 | 0.083 | 0.453*** | 0.089 |
| Navy | 30 km or less | 0.894 | 0.056 | 0.959 | 0.119 |
| | 30.1 km–60 km | (reference) | | (reference) | |
| | 60.1 km–120 km | 1.144** | 0.059 | 1.386** | 0.159 |
| | 120.1 km–240 km | 1.097 | 0.055 | 1.148 | 0.129 |
| | More than 240 km | 1.109* | 0.054 | 0.747** | 0.079 |
| **Nearest Relevant Location** | | | | | |
| Nearest MOA | 30 km or less | 1.214*** | 0.035 | 1.474*** | 0.098 |
| | 30.1 km–60 km | (reference) | | (reference) | |
| | 60.1 km–120 km | 0.974 | 0.026 | 0.793*** | 0.050 |
| | 120.1 km–240 km | 0.992 | 0.029 | 0.872* | 0.060 |
| | More than 240 km | 0.971 | 0.047 | 0.429*** | 0.061 |

## Table A.7—Continued

| Nearest Relevant Location | | (1) N(All UAPs) | | (2) N(UAPs in Clusters) | |
|---|---|---|---|---|---|
| | | IRR | SE | IRR | SE |
| Nearest IGRA weather station | 30 km or less | 0.880*** | 0.034 | 0.830* | 0.076 |
| | 30.1 km–60 km | (reference) | | (reference) | |
| | 60.1 km–120 km | 0.970 | 0.029 | 0.797** | 0.059 |
| | 120.1 km–240 km | 0.951 | 0.027 | 0.793** | 0.057 |
| | More than 240 km | 1.026 | 0.053 | 0.705* | 0.103 |
| Large civilian airport within 60 km? (1 = Yes) | | 0.822*** | 0.018 | 0.794*** | 0.044 |
| Midsize civilian airport within 60 km? (1 = Yes) | | 0.823*** | 0.027 | 0.818* | 0.069 |
| Percentage of cloudy days | | 1.015*** | 0.001 | 1.082*** | 0.003 |
| Population density (logged) | | 0.768*** | 0.006 | 0.619*** | 0.013 |
| Constant | | 0.001*** | 0.000 | 0.000*** | 0.000 |

NOTE: IRR – incident rate ratio; SE = standard error. Results were obtained from multivariate negative binomial regression models. $N = 731{,}115$. Indicator variables for years are included but not shown. Total population is included as the model exposure; its coefficient is constrained to be 1 and not shown in the table. IRRs compare rates among two different groups; an IRR of 1 is parity, an IRR < 1 indicates predicted decreases in rates, and an IRR > 1 indicates predicted increases in rates. * $p < 0.05$, ** $p < 0.01$, *** $p < 0.001$. This analysis categorized six Space Force bases in our dataset as Air Force bases.

TABLE A.8

## Associations Between UAP Sightings and Military Installations and Weather Stations

| | | (1) N(All UAPs) | | (2) N(UAPs in Clusters) | |
|---|---|---|---|---|---|
| **Nearest Military Installation** | | **IRR** | **SE** | **IRR** | **SE** |
| | 30 km or less | 0.844*** | 0.038 | 0.627*** | 0.062 |
| | 30.1 km–60 km | (reference) | | (reference) | |
| Air Force | 60.1 km–120 km | 1.003 | 0.035 | 1.113 | 0.087 |
| | 120.1 km–240 km | 1.008 | 0.035 | 0.896 | 0.071 |
| | More than 240 km | 0.873*** | 0.034 | 0.396*** | 0.036 |
| | 30 km or less | 0.807*** | 0.037 | 0.628*** | 0.074 |
| | 30.1 km–60 km | (reference) | | (reference) | |
| Army | 60.1 km–120 km | 1.049 | 0.039 | 1.776*** | 0.154 |
| | 120.1 km–240 km | 0.938 | 0.032 | 1.798*** | 0.153 |
| | More than 240 km | 0.984 | 0.037 | 1.448*** | 0.138 |
| | 30 km or less | 0.912 | 0.084 | 1.700* | 0.392 |
| | 30.1 km–60 km | (reference) | | (reference) | |
| Marine Corps | 60.1 km–120 km | 1.278** | 0.103 | 2.533*** | 0.537 |
| | 120.1 km–240 km | 1.178* | 0.086 | 3.360*** | 0.646 |
| | More than 240 km | 1.009 | 0.071 | 1.617* | 0.304 |
| | 30 km or less | 0.858** | 0.041 | 0.775** | 0.071 |
| | 30.1 km–60 km | (reference) | | (reference) | |
| Navy | 60.1 km–120 km | 0.888** | 0.036 | 0.806** | 0.067 |
| | 120.1 km–240 km | 0.970 | 0.038 | 0.706*** | 0.059 |
| | More than 240 km | 1.040 | 0.040 | 0.547*** | 0.046 |
| **Nearest Relevant Location** | | | | | |
| | 30 km or less | 0.871*** | 0.034 | 0.753** | 0.068 |
| | 30.1 km–60 km | (reference) | | (reference) | |
| Nearest IGRA weather station | 60.1 km–120 km | 0.985 | 0.029 | 0.825** | 0.060 |
| | 120.1 km–240 km | 0.974 | 0.028 | 0.887 | 0.063 |
| | More than 240 km | 1.045 | 0.054 | 0.729* | 0.106 |

## Table A.8—Continued

| Nearest Relevant Location | (1) *N*(All UAPs) | | (2) *N*(UAPs in Clusters) | |
|---|---|---|---|---|
| | IRR | SE | IRR | SE |
| Large civilian airport within 60 km? (1 = Yes) | 0.801*** | 0.017 | 0.798*** | 0.044 |
| Midsize civilian airport within 60km? (1 = Yes) | 0.816*** | 0.027 | 0.789** | 0.067 |
| Percentage of cloudy days | 1.016*** | 0.001 | 1.089*** | 0.003 |
| Population density (logged) | 0.764*** | 0.006 | 0.595*** | 0.012 |
| Constant | 0.000*** | 0.000 | 0.000*** | 0.000 |

NOTE: IRR = incident rate ratio; SE = standard error. Results were obtained from multivariate negative binomial regression models. $N = 731,115$. Indicator variables for years are included but not shown. Total population is included as the model exposure; its coefficient is constrained to be 1 and not shown in the table. IRRs compare rates among two different groups; an IRR of 1 is parity, an IRR < 1 indicates predicted decreases in rates, and an IRR > 1 indicates predicted increases in rates. * $p < 0.05$, ** $p < 0.01$, *** $p < 0.001$. This analysis categorized six Space Force bases in our dataset as Air Force bases.

TABLE A.9

## Associations Between UAP Sightings and Military Installations, MOAs, and Weather Stations, Excluding Washington and Oregon

| Nearest Military Installation | | (1) *N*(All UAPs) | | (2) *N*(UAPs in Clusters) | |
|---|---|---|---|---|---|
| | | IRR | SE | IRR | SE |
| Air Force | 30 km or less | 0.833*** | 0.038 | 0.477*** | 0.053 |
| | 30.1 km–60 km | (reference) | | (reference) | |
| | 60.1 km–120 km | 1.014 | 0.036 | 1.043 | 0.089 |
| | 120.1 km–240 km | 1.025 | 0.036 | 0.998 | 0.087 |
| | More than 240 km | 0.943 | 0.037 | 0.523*** | 0.053 |
| | 30 km or less | 0.760*** | 0.036 | 0.312*** | 0.047 |
| | 30.1 km–60 km | (reference) | | (reference) | |
| Army | 60.1 km–120 km | 1.041 | 0.040 | 1.372** | 0.133 |
| | 120.1 km–240 km | 0.910** | 0.032 | 1.472*** | 0.137 |
| | More than 240 km | 0.943 | 0.036 | 1.165 | 0.119 |
| | 30 km or less | 0.896 | 0.082 | 1.931** | 0.456 |
| | 30.1 km–60 km | (reference) | | (reference) | |
| Marine Corps | 60.1 km–120 km | 1.282** | 0.103 | 2.342*** | 0.502 |
| | 120.1 km–240 km | 1.177* | 0.086 | 3.091*** | 0.608 |
| | More than 240 km | 0.995 | 0.070 | 1.274 | 0.245 |

## Table A.9—Continued

| Nearest Military Installation | | (1) N(All UAPs) | | (2) N(UAPs in Clusters) | |
|---|---|---|---|---|---|
| | | IRR | SE | IRR | SE |
| | 30 km or less | 0.880* | 0.045 | 0.539*** | 0.068 |
| | 30.1 km–60 km | *(reference)* | | *(reference)* | |
| Navy | 60.1 km–120 km | 0.883** | 0.037 | 1.036 | 0.099 |
| | 120.1 km–240 km | 0.969 | 0.039 | 0.994 | 0.098 |
| | More than 240 km | 1.056 | 0.042 | 0.698*** | 0.067 |
| **Nearest Relevant Location** | | | | | |
| | 30 km or less | 1.176*** | 0.036 | 1.461*** | 0.116 |
| | 30.1 km–60 km | *(reference)* | | *(reference)* | |
| Nearest MOA | 60.1 km–120 km | 0.962 | 0.026 | 0.941 | 0.067 |
| | 120.1 km–240 km | 0.996 | 0.030 | 1.090 | 0.084 |
| | More than 240 km | 1.029 | 0.051 | 0.781 | 0.117 |
| | 30 km or less | 0.884** | 0.034 | 0.818* | 0.080 |
| | 30.1 km–60 km | *(reference)* | | *(reference)* | |
| Nearest IGRA weather station | 60.1 km–120 km | 1.001 | 0.030 | 0.940 | 0.073 |
| | 120.1 km–240 km | 0.979 | 0.029 | 0.786** | 0.062 |
| | More than 240 km | 1.075 | 0.057 | 0.787 | 0.125 |
| Large civilian airport within 60 km? (1 = Yes) | | 0.864*** | 0.020 | 0.902 | 0.055 |
| Midsize civilian airport within 60 km? (1 = Yes) | | 0.874*** | 0.030 | 0.844 | 0.081 |
| Percentage of cloudy days | | 1.011*** | 0.001 | 1.069*** | 0.003 |
| Population density (logged) | | 0.770*** | 0.006 | 0.616*** | 0.014 |
| Constant | | 0.000*** | 0.000 | 0.000*** | 0.000 |

NOTE: IRR = incident rate ratio; SE = standard error. Results were obtained from multivariate negative binomial regression models. $N$ = 706,007. Indicator variables for years are included but not shown. Total population is included as the model exposure; its coefficient is constrained to be 1 and not shown in the table. IRRs compare rates among two different groups; an IRR of 1 is parity, an IRR < 1 indicates predicted decreases in rates, and an IRR > 1 indicates predicted increases in rates. * $p < 0.05$, ** $p < 0.01$, *** $p < 0.001$. This analysis categorized six Space Force bases in our dataset as Air Force bases.

TABLE A.10

## Associations Between UAP Sightings and Military Installations, MOAs, and Weather Stations, Maximum Cluster Radii of 50 km and 100 km

| | | (1) N(UAPs in 50-km Clusters) | | (2) N(UAPs in 100-km Clusters) | |
|---|---|---|---|---|---|
| **Nearest Military Installation** | | IRR | SE | IRR | SE |
| | 30 km or less | 0.524*** | 0.058 | 0.599*** | 0.052 |
| | 30.1 km–60 km | (reference) | | (reference) | |
| Air Force | 60.1 km–120 km | 1.190* | 0.100 | 1.230** | 0.083 |
| | 120.1 km–240 km | 1.000 | 0.086 | 1.144* | 0.078 |
| | More than 240 km | 0.459*** | 0.046 | 0.619*** | 0.048 |
| | 30 km or less | 0.566*** | 0.071 | 0.552*** | 0.056 |
| | 30.1 km–60 km | (reference) | | (reference) | |
| Army | 60.1 km–120 km | 1.449*** | 0.132 | 1.464*** | 0.108 |
| | 120.1 km–240 km | 1.545*** | 0.139 | 1.434*** | 0.103 |
| | More than 240 km | 1.295* | 0.131 | 1.125 | 0.089 |
| | 30 km or less | 2.132** | 0.560 | 1.284 | 0.251 |
| | 30.1 km–60 km | (reference) | | (reference) | |
| Marine Corps | 60.1 km–120 km | 4.008*** | 0.978 | 2.189*** | 0.385 |
| | 120.1 km–240 km | 4.508*** | 1.026 | 2.709*** | 0.432 |
| | More than 240 km | 2.060** | 0.459 | 1.485* | 0.230 |
| | 30 km or less | 0.783* | 0.076 | 0.744*** | 0.062 |
| | 30.1 km–60 km | (reference) | | (reference) | |
| Navy | 60.1 km–120 km | 0.785** | 0.069 | 0.840* | 0.062 |
| | 120.1 km–240 km | 0.666*** | 0.059 | 0.790** | 0.057 |
| | More than 240 km | 0.539*** | 0.048 | 0.752*** | 0.054 |
| **Nearest Relevant Location** | | | | | |
| | 30 km or less | 1.471*** | 0.104 | 1.517*** | 0.084 |
| | 30.1 km–60 km | (reference) | | (reference) | |
| Nearest MOA | 60.1 km–120 km | 0.805** | 0.054 | 0.760*** | 0.039 |
| | 120.1 km–240 km | 0.920 | 0.066 | 0.832** | 0.047 |
| | More than 240 km | 0.534*** | 0.081 | 0.524*** | 0.061 |

## Table A.10—Continued

| Nearest Relevant Location | | (1) N(UAPs in 50-km Clusters) | | (2) N(UAPs in 100-km Clusters) | |
|---|---|---|---|---|---|
| | | IRR | SE | IRR | SE |
| Nearest IGRA weather station | 30 km or less | 0.813* | 0.079 | 0.640*** | 0.050 |
| | 30.1 km–60 km | (reference) | | (reference) | |
| | 60.1 km–120 km | 0.811** | 0.062 | 0.859* | 0.053 |
| | 120.1 km–240 km | 0.807** | 0.061 | 0.836** | 0.050 |
| | More than 240 km | 0.597** | 0.097 | 0.909 | 0.101 |
| Large civilian airport within 60 km? (1 = Yes) | | 1.004 | 0.060 | 0.833*** | 0.038 |
| Midsize civilian airport within 60 km? (1 = Yes) | | 0.813* | 0.075 | 0.837* | 0.059 |
| Percentage of cloudy days | | 1.093*** | 0.003 | 1.079*** | 0.002 |
| Population density (logged) | | 0.604*** | 0.013 | 0.627*** | 0.011 |
| Constant | | 0.000*** | 0.000 | 0.000*** | 0.000 |

NOTE: IRR = incident rate ratio; SE = standard error. Results were obtained from multivariate negative binomial regression models. $N = 731,115$. Indicator variables for years are included but not shown. Total population is included as the model exposure; its coefficient is constrained to be 1 and not shown in the table. IRRs compare rates among two different groups; an IRR of 1 is parity, an IRR < 1 indicates predicted decreases in rates, and an IRR > 1 indicates predicted increases in rates. * $p < 0.05$, ** $p < 0.01$, *** $p < 0.001$. This analysis categorized six Space Force bases in our dataset as Air Force bases.

TABLE A.11

## Association Between Incidents of One or More UAP Sightings in a Cluster (1 = Yes) and Military Installations, MOAs, and Weather Stations

| Nearest Military Installation | | (1) Observed CDPs with UAPs | | (2) Counterfactual CDPs with UAPs | |
|---|---|---|---|---|---|
| | | Odds Ratio | SE | Odds Ratio | SE |
| | 30 km or less | 0.796 | 0.098 | 0.990 | 0.067 |
| | 30.1 km–60 km | (reference) | | (reference) | |
| Air Force | 60.1 km–120 km | 0.995 | 0.093 | 0.992 | 0.059 |
| | 120.1 km–240 km | 0.760** | 0.071 | 0.989 | 0.058 |
| | More than 240 km | 0.373*** | 0.040 | 0.975 | 0.064 |
| | 30 km or less | 0.442*** | 0.063 | 0.928 | 0.069 |
| | 30.1 km–60 km | (reference) | | (reference) | |
| Army | 60.1 km–120 km | 1.371** | 0.140 | 1.049 | 0.068 |
| | 120.1 km–240 km | 1.381*** | 0.135 | 0.917 | 0.055 |
| | More than 240 km | 1.351** | 0.146 | 0.906 | 0.060 |
| | 30 km or less | 1.619 | 0.446 | 0.728* | 0.096 |
| | 30.1 km–60 km | (reference) | | (reference) | |
| Marine Corps | 60.1 km–120 km | 1.620 | 0.401 | 0.801 | 0.092 |
| | 120.1 km–240 km | 2.277*** | 0.518 | 0.688*** | 0.073 |
| | More than 240 km | 1.762* | 0.389 | 0.760** | 0.076 |
| | 30 km or less | 0.663** | 0.083 | 1.079 | 0.081 |
| | 30.1 km–60 km | (reference) | | (reference) | |
| Navy | 60.1 km–120 km | 0.828 | 0.084 | 0.988 | 0.067 |
| | 120.1 km–240 km | 0.585*** | 0.059 | 1.041 | 0.069 |
| | More than 240 km | 0.505*** | 0.050 | 1.065 | 0.069 |

| Nearest Relevant Location | | | | | |
|---|---|---|---|---|---|
| | 30 km or less | 1.438*** | 0.115 | 0.986 | 0.052 |
| | 30.1 km–60 km | (reference) | | (reference) | |
| MOA | 60.1 km–120 km | 0.930 | 0.069 | 0.979 | 0.044 |
| | 120.1 km–240 km | 0.872 | 0.070 | 0.939 | 0.047 |
| | More than 240 km | 0.411*** | 0.066 | 0.892 | 0.076 |

## Table A.11—Continued

| Nearest Relevant Location | | (1) Observed CDPs with UAPs | | (2) Counterfactual CDPs with UAPs | |
|---|---|---|---|---|---|
| | | Odds Ratio | SE | Odds Ratio | SE |
| | 30 km or less | 1.255* | 0.138 | 0.989 | 0.065 |
| | 30.1 km–60 km | (reference) | | (reference) | |
| Nearest IGRA weather station | 60.1 km–120 km | 0.938 | 0.079 | 0.966 | 0.051 |
| | 120.1 km–240 km | 0.867 | 0.071 | 1.063 | 0.055 |
| | More than 240 km | 0.706* | 0.114 | 1.063 | 0.102 |
| Large civilian airport | | 0.954 | 0.061 | 1.009 | 0.044 |
| Midsize civilian airport | | 0.795* | 0.077 | 1.015 | 0.066 |
| Percentage of cloudy days | | 1.077*** | 0.004 | 1.001 | 0.002 |
| Population density (logged) | | 0.940* | 0.027 | 1.019 | 0.019 |
| Total population (logged) | | 1.985*** | 0.039 | 1.710*** | 0.019 |
| Constant | | 0.000*** | 0.000 | 0.000*** | 0.000 |

NOTE: SE = standard error. Results were obtained from multivariate logistic regression models. The outcome for (1) is a binary indicator of having one or more UAP sightings in a statistically significant cluster of sightings (maximum radius = 60 km). The outcome for (2) is a binary indicator for a counterfactual sample of similarly sized CDPs to those that had at least one sighting in a UAP cluster (maximum radius = 60 km). $N$ = 731,115. Indicator variables for years are included but not shown. * $p < 0.05$, ** $p < 0.01$, *** $p < 0.001$. This analysis categorized six Space Force bases in our dataset as Air Force bases.

TABLE A.12

## Associations Between UAP Sightings and Military Installations, MOAs, and Weather Stations in Counterfactual Sample of UAP Sightings

| Nearest Military Installation | | IRR | SE |
|---|---|---|---|
| | 30 km or less | 0.988 | 0.050 |
| | 30.1 km–60 km | *(reference)* | |
| Air Force | 60.1 km–120 km | 1.003 | 0.045 |
| | 120.1 km–240 km | 1.103* | 0.049 |
| | More than 240 km | 1.082 | 0.055 |
| | 30 km or less | 0.925 | 0.052 |
| | 30.1 km–60 km | *(reference)* | |
| Army | 60.1 km–120 km | 0.956 | 0.048 |
| | 120.1 km–240 km | 0.958 | 0.044 |
| | More than 240 km | 0.950 | 0.048 |
| | 30 km or less | 1.000 | 0.098 |
| | 30.1 km–60 km | *(reference)* | |
| Marine Corps | 60.1 km–120 km | 0.945 | 0.083 |
| | 120.1 km–240 km | 0.995 | 0.081 |
| | More than 240 km | 0.928 | 0.073 |
| | 30 km or less | 0.988 | 0.054 |
| | 30.1 km–60 km | *(reference)* | |
| Navy | 60.1 km–120 km | 1.002 | 0.049 |
| | 120.1 km–240 km | 0.970 | 0.047 |
| | More than 240 km | 0.976 | 0.046 |
| **Nearest Relevant Location** | | | |
| | 30 km or less | 1.029 | 0.043 |
| | 30.1 km–60 km | *(reference)* | |
| Nearest MOA | 60.1 km–120 km | 1.018 | 0.036 |
| | 120.1 km–240 km | 1.063 | 0.040 |
| | More than 240 km | 1.029 | 0.066 |

## Table A.12—Continued

| Nearest Relevant Location | | IRR | SE |
|---|---|---|---|
| | 30 km or less | 0.968 | 0.046 |
| | 30.1 km–60 km | *(reference)* | |
| Nearest IGRA weather station | 60.1 km–120 km | 1.075 | 0.042 |
| | 120.1 km–240 km | 1.026 | 0.040 |
| | More than 240 km | 1.008 | 0.076 |
| Large civilian airport within 60 km? (1 = Yes) | | 0.823*** | 0.028 |
| Midsize civilian airport within 60 km? ( 1= Yes) | | 0.929 | 0.047 |
| Percentage of cloudy days | | 1.003* | 0.002 |
| Population density (logged) | | 0.818*** | 0.010 |
| Constant | | 0.000*** | 0.000 |

NOTE: IRR = incident rate ratio; SE = standard error. Results were obtained from multivariate negative binomial regression models. $N = 731{,}115$. Indicator variables for years are included but not shown. Total population is included as the model exposure; its coefficient is constrained to be 1 and not shown in the table. IRRs compare rates among two different groups; an IRR of 1 is parity, an IRR < 1 indicates predicted decreases in rates, and an IRR > 1 indicates predicted increases in rates. * $p < 0.05$, *** $p < 0.001$. This analysis categorized six Space Force bases in our dataset as Air Force bases.

**FIGURE A.1**

## Statistically Significant Clusters of UAP Sightings by Year

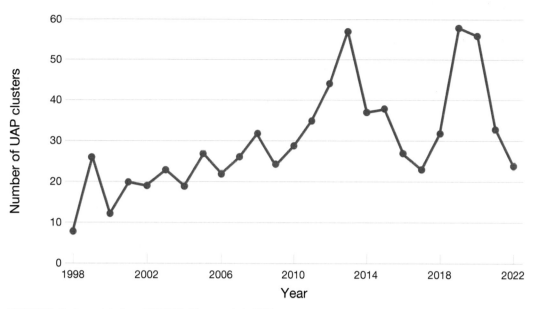

SOURCES: Features data from NUFORC; Manson et al., 2022.

FIGURE A.2

**Locations of UAP Sighting Clusters and Covariates, Including IGRA Weather Stations and Civilian Airports**

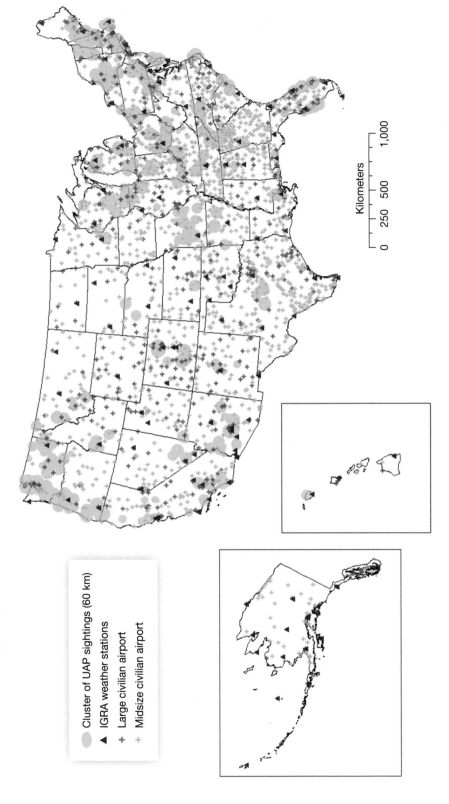

Cluster of UAP sightings (60 km)
IGRA weather stations
Large civilian airport
Midsize civilian airport

Kilometers

0   250   500   1,000

SOURCES: Presents data from NUFORC; ArcGIS Hub, 2019; National Centers for Environmental Information, undated-b.

FIGURE A.3

**Statistically Significant UAP Sighting Clusters with Maximum Radii of 50 km and 100 km**

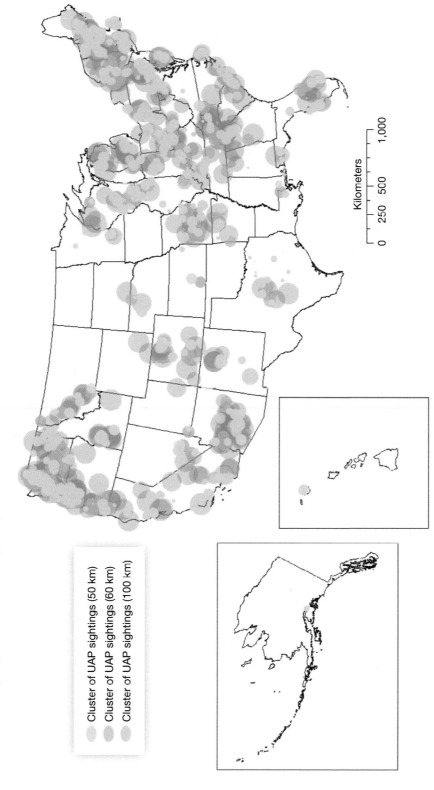

Cluster of UAP sightings (50 km)
Cluster of UAP sightings (60 km)
Cluster of UAP sightings (100 km)

Kilometers

0  250  500  1,000

SCURCES: Presents data from NUFORC; Manson et al., 2022.

# Abbreviations

| | |
|---|---|
| CDP | census designated place |
| DoD | Department of Defense |
| FAA | Federal Aviation Administration |
| IGRA | Integrated Global Radiosonde Archive |
| IRR | incident rate ratio |
| MOA | military operations area |
| NOAA | National Oceanic and Atmospheric Administration |
| NUFORC | National UFO Reporting Center |
| SE | standard error |
| SUA | special-use airspace |
| UAP | unidentified aerial phenomenon |

# References

Air University, *Doctrine Advisory: Control of the Air*, U.S. Air Force, July 2017.

ArcGIS Hub, "FAA—Airports," dataset, updated August 6, 2019. As of May 31, 2023:
https://hub.arcgis.com/documents/f74df2ed82ba4440a2059e8dc2ec9a5d/about

Chow, Denise, "To Cheaply Go: How Falling Launch Costs Fueled a Thriving Economy in Orbit," NBC News, April 8, 2022.

C-SPAN, "Hearing on Government Investigation of UFOs," video, May 17, 2022. As of March 22, 2023:
https://www.c-span.org/video/?520133-1/hearing-government-investigation-ufos

David, Leonard, "How Amateur Satellite Trackers Are Keeping an 'Eye' on Objects Around the Earth," Space.com, May 3, 2020.

Doubek, James, "Secret Pentagon Program Spent Millions to Research UFOs," NPR, December 17, 2017.

Eghigian, Greg, "Making UFOs Make Sense: Ufology, Science, and the History of Their Mutual Mistrust," *Public Understanding of Science*, Vol. 26, No. 5, July 2017.

FAA—*See* Federal Aviation Administration.

Federal Aviation Administration, "ADIP: Advanced Facility Search," database, undated-a. As of May 31, 2023:
https://adip.faa.gov/agis/public/#/airportSearch/advanced.

Federal Aviation Administration, "FAA SUA—Federal Aviation Administration," webpage, undated-b. As of March 20, 2023:
https://sua.faa.gov/sua/siteFrame.app

Federal Aviation Administration, "Chapter 15: Airspace," *Pilot's Handbook of Aeronautical Knowledge*, August 24, 2016.

Federal Aviation Administration, "Facts About the FAA and Air Traffic Control," February 4, 2020.

Federal Aviation Administration, "Chapter 25. Military Operations Areas: Section 1. General," *Order JO 7400.2P—Procedures for Handling Airspace Matters*, March 17, 2023a.

Federal Aviation Administration, "Air Traffic Plans and Publications," webpage, last modified April 20, 2023b. As of March 20, 2023:
https://www.faa.gov/air_traffic/publications/

Federal Aviation Administration, "Runway," dataset, updated April 20, 2023c. As of May 31, 2023:
https://ais-faa.opendata.arcgis.com/datasets/faa::runways/about

Federal Aviation Administration, "Special Use Airspace," dataset, updated April 20, 2023d. As of May 31, 2023:
https://ais-faa.opendata.arcgis.com/datasets/faa::special-use-airspace/about

Garamone, Jim, "F-22 Safely Shoots Down Chinese Spy Balloon off South Carolina Coast," DoD News, February 4, 2023.

Hicks, Kathleen, "Establishment of the All-Domain Anomaly Resolution Office," memorandum for senior Pentagon leadership, commanders of the combatant commands, defense agency and DoD field activity directors, Deputy Secretary of Defense, July 15, 2022.

Integrated Global Radiosonde Archive, "Station Inventory," database, version 2.2, National Centers for Environmental Information, updated January 24, 2023. As of February 24, 2023: https://www.ncei.noaa.gov/data/integrated-global-radiosonde-archive/doc/igra2-station-list.txt

Kocher, George, *UFOs: What to Do?* RAND Corporation, DRU-1571, 1968. As of April 7, 2023: https://www.rand.org/pubs/drafts/DRU1571.html

Kulldorff, Martin, "Spatial Scan Statistics: Models, Calculations, and Applications," in Joseph Glaz and N. Balakrishnan, eds., *Scan Statistics and Applications*, Birkhäuser, 1999.

Kulldorff, Martin, Farzad Mostashari, Luiz Duczmal, Katherine Yih, Ken Kleinman, and Richard Platt, "Multivariate Scan Statistics for Disease Surveillance," *Statistics in Medicine*, Vol. 26, No. 8, April 2007.

Manson, Steven, Jonathan Schroeder, David Van Riper, Tracy Kugler, and Steven Ruggles, "IPUMS National Historical Geographic Information System: Version 17.0," dataset, IPUMS, 2022. As of March 20, 2023: https://www.nhgis.org/

Military OneSource, "Military Installations," webpage, undated. As of March 20, 2023: https://installations.militaryonesource.mil/view-all

National Centers for Environmental Information, "Comparative Climatic Data (CCD)," webpage, undated-a. As of March 20, 2023: https://www.ncei.noaa.gov/products/land-based-station/comparative-climatic-data

National Centers for Environmental Information, "Data Access," webpage, undated-b. As of March 20, 2023: https://www.ncei.noaa.gov/access/search/index

National UFO Reporting Center, "File a Report," webpage, undated-a. As of May 31, 2023: https://nuforc.org/file-a-report/

National UFO Reporting Center, "The National UFO Reporting Center Online Database," webpage, undated-b. As of March 20, 2023: https://nuforc.org/databank/

National Weather Service, "NOAA Weather Radio Reception," webpage, undated. As of March 20, 2023: https://www.weather.gov/cae/reception.html

Novak, Matt, "Ukraine Military Calls on Citizens with Hobby Drones to Help Kyiv," Gizmodo, February 25, 2022.

NUFORC—*See* National UFO Reporting Center.

Office of the Director of National Intelligence, *Preliminary Assessment: Unidentified Aerial Phenomena*, June 25, 2021.

Office of the Director of National Intelligence, *2022 Annual Report on Unidentified Aerial Phenomena*, January 12, 2023.

Siegel, Julia, "Commercial Satellites Are on the Front Lines of War Today. Here's What This Means for the Future of Warfare," Atlantic Council, August 30, 2022.

Slapakova, Linda, Theodora Vassilika Ogden, and James Black, "Strategic and Legal Implications of Emerging Dual-Use ASAT Systems," *NATO Legal Gazette*, No. 42, December 2021.

Sytas, Andrius, "Turkey's Baykar Donates Drone for Ukraine After Lithuanian Crowdfunder," Reuters, June 2, 2022.

U.S. Census Bureau, "Mapping Files," webpage, undated. As of May 31, 2023:
https://www.census.gov/geographies/mapping-files.html

U.S. Census Bureau, "TIGER/Line Shapefile, 2019, nation, U.S., Military Installation National Shapefile," data files, January 15, 2021. As of May 31, 2023:
https://catalog.data.gov/dataset/tiger-line-shapefile-2019-nation-u-s-military-installation-national-shapefile

U.S. Senate Committee on Appropriations, "The People's Republic of China's High Altitude Surveillance Efforts Against the United States," video, February 9, 2023. As of March 20, 2023:
https://www.appropriations.senate.gov/hearings/oversight-on-chinese-spy-balloon

Verma, Pranshu, "Security Threat or Hot Air? A Guide to High-Altitude Balloons," *Washington Post*, February 16, 2023.

Whitaker, Bill, "UFOs Regularly Spotted in Restricted U.S. Airspace," *CBS News*, August 29, 2021.

Wilson, Bradley, Shane Tierney, Brendan Toland, Rachel M. Burns, Colby P. Steiner, Christopher Scott Adams, Michael Nixon, Raza Khan, Michelle D. Ziegler, Jan Osburg, and Ike Chang, *Small Unmanned Aerial System Adversary Capabilities*, RAND Corporation, RR-3023-DHS, 2020. As of February 24, 2023:
https://www.rand.org/pubs/research_reports/RR3023.html

Yonekura, Emmi, Brian Dolan, Moon Kim, Krista Romita Grocholski, Raza Khan, and Yool Kim, *Commercial Space Capabilities and Market Overview: The Relationship Between Commercial Space Developments and the U.S. Department of Defense*, RAND Corporation, RR-A578-2, 2022. As of February 24, 2023:
https://www.rand.org/pubs/research_reports/RRA578-2.html